Mother & Son

Marie Dullaghan

Leaf by Leaf is an imprint of Cinnamon Press
www.cinnamonpress.com

The right of Marie Dullaghan to be identified as author of this work has been asserted by her in accordance with the Copyright, Designs and Patent Act, 1988. © 2022, Marie Dullaghan

ISBN 978-1-78864-937-7

British Library Cataloguing in Publication Data. A CIP record for this book can be obtained from the British Library.

All rights reserved. No part of this publication may be reproduced, stored in a retrieval system, or transmitted in any form or by any means, electronic, mechanical, photocopying, recording or otherwise without the prior written permission of the publishers. This book may not be lent, hired out, resold or otherwise disposed of by way of trade in any form of binding or cover other than that in which it is published, without the prior consent of the publishers.

Designed and typeset in Bodoni by Cinnamon Press. Cover design by Adam Craig © Adam Craig from original artwork by Aidan Dullaghan © Aidan Dullaghan. Art work by Aidan Dullaghan © Aidan Dullaghan.

Cinnamon Press is represented by Inpress

Marie Dullaghan is retired education worker, born in Ireland, and currently living in Essex.

Since retiring she has taken up writing, with work published in *The SHOp*, (one poem republished in *The SHOp Anthology* 2020); *The High Window*; *London Grip*; *Swords Voices* and *Under the Blushing Sky* (a fund-raising anthology for victims of domestic violence).

While living in Dubai, Marie was a member of two poetry collectives: *The Poeticians*, led by Palestinian poet and film-maker Hind Shoufani; and *Punch*, run by Lebanese poet Zeina Hashem-Beck. She read/performed regularly with those collectives at various venues, including the Emirates Airline Festival of Literature.

Marie is also a passionate amateur photographer. She has had two solo photographic exhibitions, and has work published in the Middle-Eastern magazine *Sukoon,* and elsewhere.

Acknowledgements

They say it takes a village to rear a child—it takes far more than an author/artist to produce a book. I would like to make a special mention of the following people, who contributed to the development of this book:

Huge thanks to Aidan for permitting the publication of this book, which is a significant exposure of his private life at a time when he was extremely vulnerable, and for taking the time and trouble to read the manuscript fully before agreeing to publication. Thanks are also due for his incredible patience and hard work posing for the photographs, and for the very generous gift of allowing his 'juvenile' paintings to be portrayed here.

I'm extremely grateful to husband, Frank, whose constant encouragement, close editing, and general support have made the project possible.

Many thanks to Dr. Jan Fortune at Cinnamon Press for her mentorship, encouragement and the hours of editing work and to Adam Craig for his superb interior and cover design.

Gratitude to the editor of *London Grip* for publishing 'Flawed'.

In terms of Aidan's illness, I would sincerely like to thank some very special people who helped us get through those long difficult years: We were extremely fortunate to have the services of a wonderful psychiatrist, Dr. Saaliya Seneviratne, whose dedication and generosity supported us throughout. My friend, Eileen Price, always there with a listening ear, a cup of tea or a hot meal; Father Paul Fox, our parish priest, whose calmness, patience and wise advise made a huge difference; my sister-in-law, Rosemarie Kelly, for all the prayers, the phone calls, the late nights spent at her kitchen table listening to me; Helen Hopkins, who once re-arranged her entire work schedule and drove 300 miles to stay with me for a couple of days. My wonderful husband, Frank, worked himself to the bone ensuring we would be in a position to support Aidan financially beyond our own lifetime, in case he did not recover. This mission had him leaving the house before six every morning, often not returning until after eight o'clock in the evening. It took him overseas to work in Dubai where he could amass funds more quickly. It was a lonely, stressful time for us both.

The academic and administrative staff at both Seevic College in Benfleet and NSAD were truly heroic in their efforts to accommodate Aidan's 'strangeness': a tutor at his sixth form college arranged a 'sleeping place' for him behind some screens in his classroom (that sudden need for sleep caused by epilepsy); tutors tolerated his outbursts, his unexplained comings and goings in class time, the twitches and jerks and verbal tics, his irrational refusal to comply with academic norms. We are deeply grateful.

Contents

Introduction	7
Experimenting With Shamanic Ways: Events Inside a Crystal	17
I Paid No Attention	18
Metamorphosis	20
Flawed	21
Watching Through the Window	26
The Blank Canvas	28
Artist	29
Drummer	32
They Smoke Fat Cigarettes	33
Millennium Eve	34
Where Are You This Dark Night?	35
Through Smoked Glass	38
He Runs Into the Night	42
Bats Glide Overhead	44
Conversation in the Dark	45
In Those Dark Days	48
The Way Forward	49
On the Way to the Psychiatrist's Office	53
'We are the words; we are the music; we are the thing itself.'	56
Odd	60
Trainers	61
Well… It's Complicated	62
Found Poem from Charles Dickens (Pickwick Papers)	65
Lost	66
Alone on a Paper Boat	67
Stork	68
Midsummer Eve	70
Lady Ellhorn: The Elder Tree	72
Friendship Bracelet	74
Cliff Edge	75
Blackberries	76
The Sign	78
One More Day	80
Abreaction	81
The Long Haul	82
Let the Rooms Be Filled With Light	84
Image Labels	88

Introduction

I'm always reluctant to 'explain' my work—I believe it should speak for itself; but I've been persuaded that the background story is worth telling.

Early in the year 2000, when my younger son, Aidan, was sixteen, he developed Temporal Lobe Epilepsy. It manifested itself as episodic paranoid schizophrenia: hallucinations, delusions, cognitive confusion, warped logic, acute depression, loss of motivation, lack of self-care… His behaviour was often quite bizarre; and for several months he was suicidal, leading to many anxious hours waiting for him to return home from one of his long rambles.

Thankfully, Aidan now has control of his life and is married to a brilliant, courageous young woman from Manilla. They have been blessed with a son, who at the time of writing is almost a year old. Aidan is now doing invaluable work in an education setting with children who have special needs.

In spite of the difficulties, Aidan somehow managed to get through A-Levels, and a BA in Fine Arts from the Norwich School of Art and Design—an extraordinary achievement for a person in such cognitive disarray. By the time Aidan graduated, he was starting to recover, and I was attending the Cambridge School of Art, indulging a new-found interest in photography. I didn't intend to complete a full BA, (already having a degree in English Literature and Irish Language and Literature from University College Dublin, 1975) but somehow that's what happened. For my final Major Project, (summer 2009) I was advised to concentrate on portraiture, and it was suggested, on the basis of earlier work, that my best model was Aidan. Given that he was living at home, not yet working, and with little else to do, I asked him to pose for me.

Initially, I intended to do some straightforward, classical, portrait shots, but it quickly became apparent that we'd already 'done' that, and the project needed more depth. Aidan said he would be happy to continue working with me, but thought it would be more interesting if the photos were about 'both of us'. It took a long time to develop that vague notion into a full photographic project.

In trying to decide what to 'put in front of the lens' I started to explore several incidents that had occurred during the years of his illness. The conversation might start with something like 'Do you remember that time…' Aidan's memory of the event was frequently very vague, but the discussion usually brought me to a much fuller understanding of what had been happening in his head at the time. It was during these discussions that I discovered he was never sure whether he was talking to his mother, or to some evil apparition, some demon, that had come from hell to trick him. There were many startling revelations from him, and he, in turn, came to understand some of the stress and anxiety the situation had caused me. It was a very healing experience for both of us.

It was never my intention to replicate those events for the camera. The project was always 'art', not 'biography'. The intention was more to explore the emotional depths of the situations we experienced.

I decided to opt for a form of 'Constructed Image' or 'Staged Photograph' to re-imagine the narratives, using some element that we both recognised, without attempting historical accuracy. I spent many hours considering the details: what space to use (I discovered we were at our best inside our own home), whether there should be any furniture in the images, what that should look like, where it should be positioned; and what we should wear, particularly what colours. There was much re-arranging of rooms!

Mostly, I chose to keep the light quite dim; through the whole course of the illness we were more or less 'travelling blind'.

Although I shoot digital, I'm not at all comfortable with 'tech', and used a fairly basic DSLR camera. I had no fancy gadgets to enable remote shooting; I placed the camera on a tripod, framed the shot, and relied on the camera's timer to let me get into the frame.

There were two sequences where I needed a spare pair of hands—a volunteer to actually click the shutter. Only one such is included in this book, and the camera operator is acknowledged.

The completed photographic project contained about thirty images, most of them in pairs or triplets.
After graduation, and back in Dubai, I was invited to exhibit the work in a local art gallery. This led to an invitation to stage the exhibition again in Dubai's Zayeed University.
I also entered the project in the World Photography Organisation's annual competition, where it got an 'honorable mention' in the 'Deeper Perspectives' category (2010).

When the second exhibition ended we wrapped the prints and stored them in our Dubai apartment. By that time, I was accompanying my husband, Frank, to poetry readings. He's been writing for decades. It didn't take me long to want to join in. That meant writing poems. I'm sure the early ones were rather awful, but the group (The Poeticians) led by Hind Shoufani was very accepting, and I became accustomed to reading on the open mic. Later I joined a new group called Punch, led by Lebanese poet, Zeina Hasem-Beck. I came to love the monthly readings.

The photographs might never have seen the light of day again if it hadn't been for shh!... l-o-c-k-d-o-w-n.
When the COVID outbreak began we were in Kuala Lumpur, one last work project for husband Frank before retirement. In Malaysia, when they say 'lockdown' they mean it—no daily walk for exercise, no travelling to the shopping mall, no mixing. Grocery shopping was to be done in the nearest supermarket by one adult per household once a week. In temporary accommodation (luxurious though it was) we had none of our usual resources. No art equipment, no musical instruments, a very limited supply of books. Frank was busy with administrative and accounting work, so there were long hours of silence. And there's only so many hours you can spend dusting a minimalist apartment. I started getting really serious about the poetry…

There was already the germ of an idea about making a digital presentation of the images to present at festivals, or at mental health awareness days. So I now tried to develop some writing to accompany the presentation. For most of that time, however, my laptop was stuck in the repair shop and I had no access to the photos. This was probably an advantage, forcing me to take a fresh approach to the remembered experience. The writings in this book are not, therefore, descriptions or explanations of the images. They are what Wordsworth would have called 'emotion recollected in tranquility'.

Since returning to the UK I have been mentored by Dr. Jan Fortune of Cinnamon Press. The initial aim was to sort through my poetry files and see whether I had anything of value, try to figure out what role writing (poetry, short story, drama) might have in my future. Of course, I had a particular interest in developing work on the 'Mother and Son' theme.

With Jan's help, and significant editorial assistance from Frank, I have now blended the photographs and writing into a single art-book.

I have not included all the images from the original series, nor, of course, all my writing on the subject. The pieces have been chosen for quality, variety, narrative integrity and the way they resonate together.

The book includes a few photos of artwork produced by Aidan during the years of his illness. I have included them where I think they add depth to the project as a whole. I want to be clear that the paintings were entirely separate from the photos and the writing. The paintings were finished long before either the photographs or the writing were even imagined.

I am deeply grateful to Aidan for allowing me to use that artwork. I would like to thank him properly for all his hard work as a photographic model (you have no idea how much patience he needed!). I am even more grateful that he has given his full permission to publish the project, to tell our story to anyone who might come across the book. It is surely evidence, if any more were needed, that his days of paranoia are firmly in the past.

I hope you find something of interest in this book and that it may perhaps help you in understanding your own or someone else's mental health experiences. If you are a carer, as anxious as I was, may it bring you hope.

Marie Dullaghan, 14th January 2022

Poetry sheds no tears 'such as Angels weep,' but natural and human tears...
its object is truth... carried alive into the heart by passion... it is as immortal
as the heart of man... poetry is the spontaneous overflow of powerful feelings:
it takes its origin from emotion recollected in tranquillity

> William Wordsworth

Dedicated to my two amazing sons, Fergus and Aidan and their extraordinary wives, Lynsey and Louise.

Mother and Son

Experimenting With Shamanic Ways: Events Inside a Crystal

Self-induce a trance... slide inside the quartz... to a landscape that could be North Wales, or the Wye Valley... stroll the woodland path that might be familiar.

Rabbit lifts his head, sniffs; bounds towards me, curious.
He sits on his haunches, stares; blinks. Vanishes.
Moments later he is running alongside—
watchful, knowing eyes. So fast, down the trail ahead,
puffball tail bouncing up, down, up, down.

I follow the path back, knowing to leave by the way
I entered. Rabbit waits by the gate. Asks: *where are you going?*
I tell him *home*. He says: *Wrong gate. You came
in down there.* I think he's lying, telling some trickster tale
for his own purposes. *Go that way if you want;*
he shrugs. *You will find yourself... someplace else.*

Confused, I follow where he points. He is right, of course.
There's that red berried bush, that patch of bare rock,
the clump of yellow flowers. Now I see my gate;
and there he is again, waiting. *Take me with you.*
It is more command than request. I tell him 'No.
I'm not supposed to take anything from here.'

*I'm coming anyway. I can do that. You won't like it
if I come by myself. Better for you to bring me.*
He's making me nervous. I refuse; tell him to wait,
that I will check what's allowed, maybe come back for him.
He laughs; a cruel snarl of a laugh. *Too late*, he says.
You had your chance, you only get one chance.

Remember that when we meet again...

I rise from somewhere deep, deep, through a fuddle of dark.
Reclining in my armchair; the quartz crystal clasped in my hand.
I check the room, make sure I'm home, in the right place; check
if Rabbit is hiding somewhere in the house, the garden. He is not.

Months pass and I forget. Then one winter's day
I hear that snarling laugh. I see him. I know him.
Rabbit—Ruler of my son's deranged mind.

I Paid No Attention

He was quiet, headphones glued to his ears;
rarely smiled.
He spent hours staring: a spot on the floor, a teaspoon,
the curtains...

He developed a liking for salads, raw vegetables,
especially carrots.
He ate them unpeeled, unwashed even,
refused meat.

Times he would hunker down on the floor,
raise his head
and sniff at the air, as if checking whether someone was
making fresh coffee.

One afternoon, we met a dog; it barked, growled,
hackles raised:
The lad was not surprised. *Didn't you know? I'm a rabbit;
prey of dogs, cats, large birds.*

I never saw long ears, little white tail or whiskers growing. But then
all unprepared,
I was a new rabbit's mother. It was time to learn about burrows, time
to pay attention.

Metamorphosis

He was old enough. I didn't need to be on his case. Found
space for books and film; for the guitar; *me* time.

the mother pays very little attention to her young.

He could fix his own lunch: sandwiches, pizza, chips.
I ignored the empty beer cans.

a good pet, doesn't require much care

He spent his days in his bedroom, slipped out at dusk
to walk a few miles—an artist's creative isolation.

almost nocturnal, usually solitary

He hid his ears under headphones, said little.
Our conversations grew out of step with each other.

has no speech, gives warnings by thumping a foot on the ground

I barely noticed the change in diet—the carrots and spinach,
lettuce and dandelions; the boiled nettles, the plates of herbs.

voracious plant eater

Then that day he dashed from the garden,
the neighbour's dog barking at his heels,

nervous and highly-strung

to hide, a twitching bundle of body,
under blankets piled on his bed.

an exceptionally vulnerable mammal

I knew it was time to get a grip,
understand this metamorphosis.

Rabbit: long-ears… family Leporidae… lives about nine years

Flawed

He calls himself 'Rabbit', nibbles lettuce,
watches her from under the table.

She has been baking bread for days,
or weeks, maybe. Tray after tray.

The pickled oranges stare
at the apple chutney.

The loaves are every shade of brown
from almond cream to jasper black,

but some are tasteless, heavy,
too much salt or sugar. She could do better.

Among the cherries a solitary grape
screams 'green' in the white fruit bowl.

She frets. No one will love her
imperfect bread. Better stick to scones.

In its cardboard nest, one of her eggs is cracked.

Watching Through the Window

The art assignment is overdue; he promises to paint today…
I leave him in the studio, mixing colours.

Three hours later
he still stands by the blank canvas.

Again and again he rolls the brush between finger and thumb,
examines the bristles… dips in the almost dry paint on his palette.

Of a sudden, his brush makes a stab towards the canvas,
snatches back without touching, falls from his hand.

He has not seen me.

He breathes like an old man on a ventilator,
squirms, moans like an animal in pain.

Where his brush falls,
the floorboards will forever hold the stain of amber paint.

The Blank Canvas

It's their eyes.
Paint gets in. It hurts them.
I think it kills them. Those people,
the people in the other world.

When I close my eyes I can still
see them. They're there. Look!
They're staring at you. Their eyes
are red. They're so miserable.

All over the canvas. Everywhere.
I'm frightened. I don't want to hurt them,
but the paint kills them. I can't paint.

You don't understand. It would kill them.
You don't believe—you can't see them,
but they're real;
        it would be murder.

Artist

I search the silent classrooms

before the caretaker locks the doors,

find him at his easel in the art room,

headphones locking the voices

in, or out, of his head,

watch while ink bleeds from his brush,

his demons staining the canvas black.

Drummer

Stand beside him—outside—watch
as he climbs into his dark. Touch his arm,
see—he jerks as if your hand chars his skin.
Call his name: he will not answer.
Call him again. Understand, he does know
who you are, or even if you are...

You cannot hear his voice, his heart
—breath—nothing—until he hammers
that tattoo of terror on his birthday drums.
Drums you bought when he was still
a normal son.

                    Now you hear him. Oh yes—
bottles rattle from crates
                    paintings jump from walls
sofa thumps the floor
                    windows vibrate—
Your bones shake,
                    might break into flakes of dust.

They Smoke Fat Cigarettes

Love is a reindeer's horn,
he says, then
Mum, I'm afraid.

I stop day-dreaming;
get a familiar tune on the radio—
jazz—

He uncorks wine bottles,
spills red into the sand
until all I can do is laugh.

Do not interrupt
the moonlit landscape
with your noise.

A gull's feather falls:
Manna for us hungry folk
sitting soft among cushions.

Orion's shape above the clouds
advances, retreats. *See, the stars*
dance like drunken circles.

Later, a crowd of strangers
gathers. They have come to pray
for a little girl lost to the waves—

their words of grief
drift on hopeful lanterns,
ablaze in the night sky.

No one listens. No one sees.
Even the moon has hidden
its face, slammed the door.

On hands and knees he crawls
where waves wet the sand;
examines small pebbles—

a child searching for a lost treasure.

Millennium Eve

We make no plans, but a last minute invitation
brings us to a pub party, just before midnight.

Loud greetings, shouting to be heard. Someone
thrusts a glass into my hand: *just in time*, he yells.

I feel the phone vibrate in my pocket; consider
whether to bother—but it might be the troubled son.

It is his friend's mother. *Have you seen them?
Do you know where they went?* I hear her terror.

Her boy is suicidal, left home with my lad.
Neither seen for hours. Phones unanswered.

My throat tightens, gut clenches. Air will
not enter my lungs. The countdown begins.

I search the crowd for my husband, cannot
see him. Six…five…four…three…two…one.

Someone is hugging me tight, then someone else,
another, and another. I swing back and forth,

am swept into the circle—Auld Lang Syne—
forward, back, arms pumped up, arms down, the tune

goes on and on, ends in applause, laughter,
a downing of drinks. I grab my husband's hand

drag him out the door. Run for the car—
We have to find them. We have to
                                            find them.

Where Are You This Dark Night?

I call and call but you do not come.

I could leave the safety of my own sane mind,
follow you through the tangled maze
of your thoughts,
to where the moon makes of clouds
an ink on canvas monochrome,
where shifting nimbi change the landscape
moment by moment.
I could step out in spite of my fear
of travelling blind,
in spite of knowing how easy
it is to get lost;
knowing that in your desert a whole camel train
of helpers might pass within yards,
unseen—
leaving us abandoned among the dunes,
where soon
the inevitable scorching sun would come
to leach the life from our bodies,
leave us skin-burnt, parched, dry as the sand.

If I take the risk, will you answer me?

Through Smoked Glass

My third eye sees you sometimes, dark, distorted,
as if I watch through a barrier of foggy glass.

Out there, the land is full of dips and hollows,
caves and hills. You drop into the valleys out of sight.

I scour the land for a glimpse of you, watch
for your head to poke over some unlikely hillock,

some random tuft of grass—and there you are—
above ground, startled; eyes darting from place to place

ready to flee.

I remember you aged six, how you wandered off;
the whole scout-camp was in an uproar—the search.

You went to explore the man-made caves that should
have been locked. Got lost in there.

Our astonishment when your carrot-coloured hair
popped up, briefly—air vent too narrow for an escape.

They had to coax you along the passages,
shining a torch through the entrance to guide you.

And now, there is no obvious entrance or exit. I cannot
map a route out for you. If only I could shine a light…

I watch through my third eye; try to follow your path.
I think, I hope, I want to believe that you've come a little closer.

He Runs Into the Night

Now he leaps from the car,
before it quite stops;
uncoils his long body and races
across the flood-plain in the night.

I cannot see the demons
that chase him,
but perhaps a blacker shape
follows him through the darkness.

I can tell when they catch up
with him—his shriek fills
the emptiness where he
used to play football with his mates.

A wolf howl, heart-stopping wail,
ice-water in my veins.
On and on. Dogs take up his call.
Until the thud of silence.

Bats Glide Overhead

silent as his demons, waiting

for the moment he steps

too close to the otherworld,

when they will close in,

bind him, steal him from me—

steal him from himself.

Conversation in the Dark

Why did you run, son?
What was in your head?

        Go away, go home! Leave me…

It's cold here, and damp,
you haven't brought a coat.

        Go away, go home! Leave me…

Come with me to the fireside,
you know you love the flames.

        Go away, go home! Leave me…

Coffee, beer, a sandwich,
an Indian takeaway?

        Go away, go home! Leave me…

Please, please won't you tell me

        Go away, go home! Leave me.
        It's better you don't know.
        Go away, go away! GO AWAY!

In Those Dark Days

When the future was a void
yawning at our feet
I stayed close and called your name.

When Rabbit yoked your spirit
and dogs snarled at your heels
I barked those hounds away.

When you were demon-hunted
and tried to hide your face
I shouted childhood prayers.

When your mind
was a smoking torment
I took you swimming in the lake.

When shadows laughed at you
I said they laughed at me
and told a dozen stupid jokes.

When your speech was lost
to senseless mouthings
I guess-read your loose-wired brain.

When you slept, I spent long hours
in prayer: *let my efforts be enough*.
Thank God. It was enough.

The Way Forward

Doubt eats my mind
not as a python swallows
you whole, digests internally,

not as a crocodile destroys
with sudden clamp of jaw,

nor as a shark devours
all teeth and bite and rip and shred,

not as a woodpecker pecks
prods, pokes, pulls

nor as a mouse neatly nibbles

but as a greedy goat
relentlessly grazes, denudes…

the earth bare, until
all the pathways disappear.

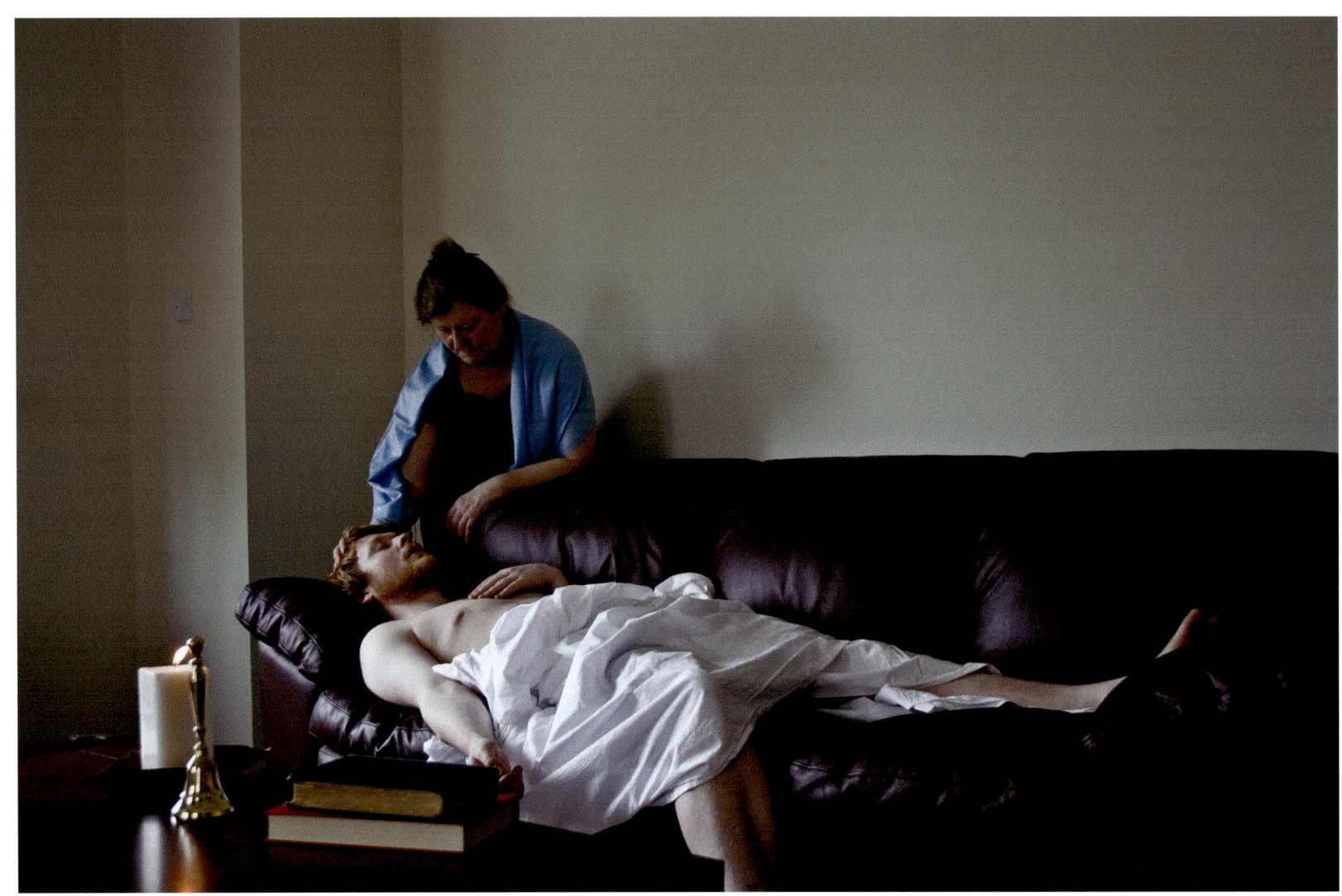

On the Way to the Psychiatrist's Office

Some stories are never told. Often we are completely oblivious to the novels being written by people around us. Sometimes we observe a mere sentence or two from a chapter; but all the time, all around us, stories are happening. Like this one:

My son was tired, muttering to himself as he trailed along behind me. 'Coffee?' I suggested. 'There's a Costa on the corner.'

I waited while the words penetrated, till he looked up. 'No!' Sharp. Peremptory. The 'not negotiable' voice.

But at least I had his attention. 'There's soft armchairs. We could wait in there.'

He frowned, pushed past me. Lurched towards a metal street seat situated at the junction, its back to the main road, facing down the side street. He slumped down at one end, waved me towards the other. I said nothing, kept my expression neutral, a skill I had developed during these last few years. Reluctantly, I sat down beside him.

He must be freezing I thought, looking at the ancient velour jacket, the shirt with a button missing, the shredded jeans... and those holed trainers.

I could feel the chill myself, even through the heavy coat, scarf, jumper, boots. The rain was light but steady. I had no idea what to do. We still had nearly two hours to wait, and he refused all cover.

I took a few deep, slow, breaths. 'Sorry, Mum. Sorry.' He seemed to be sobbing, but it could be shivering from cold. I took off my scarf and wrapped it awkwardly round his shoulders. He was so much bigger than me. 'Nice', he murmured, then 'sleep'.

He bent sideways, placing his head on my lap, curling his long legs until he was lying along the seat. I started to open the buttons on my coat; by the time I was finished, he was as sound asleep as an infant. I groaned softly, covered as much of us both as I could with my coat, its wide skirt.

I could feel the hairs at the nape of my neck rising, that 'someone is watching me' signal that is never wrong. I fumbled a folded umbrella from my handbag, securing the bag between his body and mine. Surreptitiously, under the opening umbrella, I examined the surroundings.

The main street behind me was busy enough, a constant stream of cars in both directions, a couple of push-bikes, plenty of pedestrians. A few yards away, a young man in leathers was parking a motorbike, taking his time about removing his helmet. I watched him for a while. Nothing unusual about him, and he never once glanced my way. Him? No, not him, but there were still eyes on me. I could feel them. And then I saw him. The man in the hooded parka across the road, walking slowly down the pavement, head down and shoulders hunched. He wasn't looking now, but I knew it was him. I remembered seeing that warm parka walking the other direction down the footpath when we arrived. Perhaps he too was waiting for someone, pacing, wishing he had claimed the seat before we arrived. Poor chap. He was out of luck now.

I settled back, closing my eyes. The lad was heavy on my knees. My feet would have pins and needles before I could get moving—there it was again, that tingling on the back of my neck. I wished parka man would go away. I turned awkwardly to look at him, stare him out—but he still had his back turned on his way down the street. Where were the eyes then?

A slow sweep of the neighbourhood—there, in the hotel doorway about twenty yards down the side street. A balding, middle aged man, rolling a cigarette, but every now and again looking directly towards me. Too far away to catch his eye, to question his attention. I adjusted the coat around us both. The lad's head was getting heavier on my legs. I tried to relax, planned what I would tell the shrink when we finally got to his office.

Twenty minutes later the hairs were rising on the back of my neck again.

Something was going down here, they were still watching me. Parka-Man was back, leaning against a lamp-post across the street, directly behind me. BaldySmoker was still observing me, and examining the street in detail, trying to look casual. I shifted, twisting awkwardly to sit sideways on the seat, so I could keep an eye on them both.

Nothing much changed during the next half-hour, except that my legs grew numb, and I was getting bitterly cold. I tried to wake the boy up, but he had obviously had an 'episode' that I wasn't aware of. Epilepsy will do that—a minor, barely noticeable seizure, and he'd be in a deep sleep for hours. There was only an hour to go now till his appointment, and it would be difficult to wake him, get him moving. In desperation, I phoned my husband. His office was nearby, the main reason we were in this area. He was just leaving now and would be with us in a few minutes.

I searched my bag for high-carb treats. Sometimes the smell of food would wake him. Well… a bacon sandwich might, but chocolate and crisps were unlikely to help. Still, I tried. I jiggled my knees and held the open pack of crisps under his nose. After a few minutes, there was a slight movement of the head, a faint flicker of the eyelids. I worked the crisp pack harder, and—

Something was happening.

A woman, wearing a bright yellow scarf, stood a few yards away. I thought she was considering an approach. BaldySmoker tensed, tossed his cigarette (surely not the same one) onto the pavement and hurried towards us. Parka-Man stepped into the road, forcing a white car to brake sharply; the driver honked the horn. It was all go now, and I wished the boy would wake up, get off me. I called his name, urgently. The woman took a few steps towards me, but stopped suddenly when she heard the horn. She noticed Parka-Man, turned quickly and hurried down the side street. She shook her head at BaldySmoker, and he too turned, racing to the hotel door and inside.

Parka-Man chased after the woman, muttering urgently into his jacket sleeve; then hesitated, turned to look at us again. He seemed undecided whether to proceed or return. At that moment, my husband arrived, running, umbrella held high to avoid hitting anyone in the face, briefcase banging against his knee. Later, he said he didn't know why he was running. He thought maybe we needed him to come fast. Parka-Man was obviously staring at us now, and I pointed him out to my husband, who dropped his briefcase, folded the umbrella, and got ready for a confrontation. Parka-Man lowered his head and walked off at a very past pace, disappearing from view at the bottom of the side street.

Some stories are never told… but all the time, all around us, stories are happening.

Sometimes, when I'm half asleep, I relive that scene. I don't know what that story was about. I don't know what might have happened, almost happened, didn't happen, that night—but the hairs on the back of my neck are never wrong. I was in the middle of a story.

'We are the words; we are the music; we are the thing itself.'

Virginia Woolf

I search the dictionary for words to bring you back;
there must be some spell or prayer that can pierce your fear.
Nothing works.
For a while it seemed that music might help—
but your favourite songs are those that drive us deeper,
disturbing lyrics from half-mad pessimists,
Radiohead, Jamiroquai, and the rest.
Only Mozart's K448 blocks your eruptions—
but you resist, hide my CD…

No sound from voice or instrument can bring relief;
no promises, no words of care—
no peaceful piano, no perfect harmony—
You do not heed words of love, you need
the thing itself. You and me—mother to son.

Odd

The twelve-year-old version,
reclining on a rug, torso propped
against pillows as he stared at the fire;
slipper-sock on each foot,
hand-knitted by his friend's grandmother—
one blue, the other a dull rainbow.

The right foot is not the same as the left,
because it is the right.
The left foot is not the same as the right,
because it is the left.
Nobody should expect them to dress the same,
just because they're both feet.
Let them make their own
choices. Don't judge them.

Trainers

Old—
they should have been binned years ago.
There is one shoe for the right foot
and one for the left. They do not match.

Sole—
almost detached from the upper. It flaps
when he walk, a mouth opening and closing.
He gags it with gaffer tape.

Well... It's Complicated

When might Mum be planning to buy him new shoes?

I glance at his feet. Sigh.
Where are they, son? Don't you like them any more?

They're happy under the bed.
Safely wrapped in white tissue in their box.
They were comfortable there.
I love them. They're beautiful. Soft. Clean.
Innocent.
I couldn't drag them out in the cold and wet and dirt.
And besides, these old friends would feel
betrayed, abandoned, if I left them behind.

I try to catch the psychiatrist's eye, make
that 'what can I do with him' hand gesture.
He stares at my son, tilts his head
a little to the side, eyebrows raised.
hmm... he says, at last. *Perhaps,*
we can talk about shoes next time...

He has an old pair of trainers. Well, they're not a pair, exactly - just two very old trainers, one for the right foot and one for the left. They should have been thrown out years ago, but I could no more bin the trainers than I could steal a comfort blanket form a toddler; he is unreasonably attached to them.

I have long since ceased to be embarrassed by the glances of strangers or the questions of acquaintances.

It does not matter that the right-foot sole has parted from the upper, making a flapping mouth that opens and closes with every step, nor that the left-foot sole has a gaping hole allowing sharp stones to pierce his skin.

It does not matter that his feet get cold, get wet, get cut and hurt.

The trainers are his friends, and he will never part with them.

I told him they were a work of art and should be framed. "Maybe," he said. "Maybe they are becoming art. Maybe someday they can be framed.

Roll on that day! I could live with the trainers in a glass case - but for now I just keep thinking that they're the most malodorous pair of friends I've ever met!

Found Poem from Charles Dickens (Pickwick Papers)

He cowered in obscure corners
the cold dew of fear
stood in large drops on his skin

Who saw the tears
steal down my cheeks?

Old spirits whispered—
taunted him
sly and jeering faces
rioted in his consciousness
screamed into his head
till the room rang

strange beings flocked around him
he rolled upon the ground with shrieks

straight and swift he ran
no one dared to stop him
he fled,
borne upon the arms of demons
who swept along on the wind.

Who saw me tear my hair?

Moons rays, slowly stealing in
served only to show
the dark shadows about him

long, long years of restless nights
and dreadful dreams
it seemed that so it had always been
and so it would ever be.

It makes me cold to remember.

Lost

In the space between pillow and sleep
I watch the moon drip water

from the bottom of its curve as if
it were melting into the ocean.

An old wooden pier scatters its planks
from under my racing feet.

I kneel on a surfboard, paddle through fog,
listen for your voice calling.

There is no sun, no moon, no beacon,
in the darkness. Nothing to follow

except the sounds of your fear. Hold on.
I'm coming. I will follow wherever you go.

Alone on a Paper Boat

in a sea that's never kind
to soggy ships;
rudderless and blown
this way and that,
tugged by the tide
of medical advisors,
pushed by opinionated
friends who know nothing,
crushed by a squall of judgement
from critical strangers,
steered by the thin strand
of hope that comes and goes
—moonlight on a cloudy night:
this lonely boat
fragile, barely floating,
but still the best,
the only
life raft you'll find in this storm.

There are times when I know—
paper boats are no use;
times when I would climb
the paper sail
to get above the rising seas,
times I yell
for a balloon, a bird, a cloud—
anything that could
snatch me up,
          get me out of here.

Stork

Birds have their own habits. Storks, we know, are very distinctive, with their penchant for delivering babies and standing on one leg; and did you know they eat small birds and mammals as well as frogs, fish and insects? I should study storks. They might help me understand:

He stands on one leg, stares at the floor.
An hour passes; another. I call him
every few minutes, but he doesn't
seem to hear. Nothing breaks his focus.

He has begun to wobble. Soon he
will fall, crash to the floor. *Please,*
I say, *please put your foot down.*
Fat drops of sweat plop on the tiles.

I stand in front of him, yell his name.
He does not hear, does not see me.
I take his head between my hands.
His eyes startle, meet mine.

What are you doing? I ask. His eyes
search the floor. A sob shakes his body.
Then, all of a sudden, he runs;
charges through the door to the street.

His friends search the town, all the usual
haunts: the pub, the bandstand, the park.
He is asleep under an ash tree, light from
the setting sun peering through its cleft.

Years later he explains: *there were babies
on the floor, thousands of them, piled
together, crushing each other. I could not
take a step without killing…*

*… I was trying to choose, where to put
a foot that would do the least damage.
I could not see a way. When I saw you,
they disappeared, but only for a moment.*

*Before I reached the door, my feet
trampled so many. I could feel
the squish of them under my shoes.
So many babies. Did I kill the babies?*

Midsummer Eve

When I was a kid I broke a mirror. I knew
the bad luck would stay
for seven years. I cried for hours.

Mum told me I could put the bad luck
into a stone, then throw it in the river,
let the water wash it away.

Evil is worse than bad luck.
It might spread everywhere.
Water touches everything.

But there's a tree. There's a lady in the tree.
She smiles, like a mother.
I put my hands on the trunk, send all

the evil through the bark.
The tree just soaks its up…
Peace, at last.

I must have been asleep for hours.

Daylight, sunshine! But here under the tree all is dark.
All around the tree, darkness, darkness.

The lady looks so ill.
What have I done? Let me take it back…

but evil has taken the whole tree.
My hands cannot pull it back out.

The Lady is weak. She cannot
expel it. She swallowed it. It swallowed her.

I should have been stronger.
It was my burden to carry, and now

I have destroyed the lady.
Now, I have a new burden to carry.

Lady Ellhorn: The Elder Tree

This is the tree they call *Medicine Chest*;
with country folks' cures for coughs and colds,
for rheumatism, age-wrinkled skin, or wounds,
for sprains, inflammations, allergy-puffed eyes.

This is the tree to make cordials and wine,
salads from buds and fritters from flowers.
You can cook the berries in jams and pies,
but be careful with roots and bark.

This is the tree that makes colours and dyes,
purple-blue berries, yellow-green leaves,
grey-black from wood. Make combs from branch,
or fixings for thatch, pegs and pipes and toys.

This is the tree to grow by the dairy
to keep milk from turning sour;
hang a branch at the door of the stable
to keep the horses safe from flies.

This is the tree gives me hollow branches
for whistles and pipes and tunes faeries love.
A tree for the thrill-seekers, those
a bit wild, a tree for the lover of freedom.

This is the tree for beginnings and endings,
the crossing of thresholds; a guard at the door
between this world and next. Some say
it brings death if you take it inside.

This is the tree that removes evil enchantments
cast upon folks by wizard or witch.
Carry a twig with you for luck, but
be generous…

This is the tree designed for protection,
to keep the land safe from evil and harm;
a tree full of healing that tries to keep
madness away from human minds.

This is the tree my son ran to touch
to pour out the evil he felt in his head;
the tree that welcomed his frightened fingers
and offered him kindness, watched over his sleep.

Friendship Bracelet

It falls apart;
false-gold thread unwinds
from paper beads.

Dark nutshells crack.
Thin coats of bright paint erode,
expose their true under-layers.

Metal hoops bend and twist,
surfaces stained and scratched.
They were never fit for purpose.

The elastic thread is ready to snap.
It was always weak, flawed,
unreliable—I can see that now.

Cliff Edge

Wind tugs me to the edge where
rain-wet grass gives way to hard rock.

I stand—an extinguished lighthouse—
on the cold cliff under ashen skies.

Below, angry seas hurl
onto the shore, rise in fuming spray,

fall back again and again, beating the rocks
into ever-sharper swords, points upward.

I feel insubstantial as air, invisible
as a shadow on a sunless day. Surely, no-one

would notice me topple and fall, my spirit
joining the wind. The sea can take care of the rest.

Blackberries

Weather-perfect summer day, and nothing to do that can't wait until tomorrow. It should be restful, but here I am, a black hole on a sun-lounger in the garden. He leans against the patio door, watching me. Or maybe not watching me—perhaps seeing nothing at all, or something that isn't there. *Don't try to guess.*

Eventually, a question bursts forth: *If I bring tea will you drink it?* Aggressive. A challenge of some sort—there doesn't have to be a reason. *Don't react.* A deep sigh gives me breath for speech, although it doesn't generate energy. *Yes. Okay. If you would like to bring it.* *Stay passive, non-argumentative.* Soon he is standing between me and the sun, mug of tea in hand, staring at me. He does not attempt to hand the mug over. *Am I supposed to say please?*

Lightbulb flash in his eyes of an idea crossing his mind. An indistinct murmur, a nod of his head. He hooks my table with his foot, moves it away. *Why?*

There! Triumphant. He places the drink on the table, now just out my reach. Steps back; watches to see what I'll do. *What's going on in his head now?*

Thanks. I half-rise, stretch to pick up the mug, praise the perfect ratio of milk to tea. *Lovely.* *Pretend it's normal. Don't notice the deliberate inconvenience.* **Oh! It really is you.** He mutters to himself for a minute, something about demons in the sunshine. *Never sure,* he ends. *Don't ask. It won't make sense.*

Mum… Quiet. Anxious. Uncertain, he places his hand on my arm, moves to stand behind me, massages my shoulders. *He hasn't done that since… forever.*

I know something's wrong. Is it me? Can I fix it? Nothing will fix my world. All broken—son, parents, sisters, and now friends. *Careful what you tell him.* **Mum, if anything in the world was possible right now, what would make it better?** *Don't tell him how badly they treated you—it could be dangerous.*

It's not your fault, son. Just life. You're right. I should do something cheerful. Maybe collect blackberries before I clip that bramble. Make jam. *Distract him.* He seems excited. Gets a basket, starts gathering fruit. *He'll be disappointed.* **You do know the jam probably won't happen, son!** *Manage expectations.*

Of course not! He laughs. *You don't even know how… Pretend, Mum. Let's just pretend.*

Even in the depths of his own darkness, he had seen my light go out.

The Sign

Tapping at the driver's window. I ignore it, fight
the tears, silence my sobs. Beside me the lad
stares at the horizon. Still the tapping.

And I look.

Brown seeds, in arcs and curves, graduating
from dark centre to the fringe of yellow petal,
slapping its whole face against the car window.

Jesus Christ! The words startle out.

A soft chuckle, a multiplicity of simultaneous
responses: *At your service, my dear!*
and *Not exactly, but close enough!*

with: *Who else would it be?*
also: *You know it's hard to get your attention!*
then: *You prayed for a sign, will this do?*

Honks from behind force me to drive on.

Now I know for sure—I am totally insane,
hearing the voice of God in my head. Or
was it… a talking sunflower, laughing at me.

Hallucination! Hallucination!

But there in front of me, beaming from the verge:
another two massive blooms, leaning into the traffic,
waving like a man hailing a taxi.

Believe! they shout. *Believe!*

One More Day

This is how we survive,
one day at a time—
and it's good to end one day,
to bury its pain
in the darkness of night,
before the next day begins.

Abreaction

I've been piling on the pressure. I want to know WHY he hates
himself. He asks me to drive, and I do, even through this awful
storm. *I'll tell you now. Stop now.* Dual carriageway. Tyres screech
into the first lay-by. Hazards flashing.
His fists pound the dashboard, feet kick the cover from the wiring. He
sobs like a hysterical toddler, barely able to speak:
even… why you still care… only…
a mother… could… mother… love…
You don't know me… evil. I'm evil.

Will he leap from the car, run into traffic, under a truck? Lock the
doors.

You'll hate me when I tell you. But you won't stop asking. Why you
can't just leave it alone— I-don't-want-you-to-hate-me.

He's losing it. Out of control. Who knows what might happen…
Release the seatbelt; unlock my door, hold it slightly ajar. Be ready
to move—to jump out. But what then?
I promise: I will never hate you. No matter what.

Words are falling over themselves, choking in the bottleneck of his
throat; bursting from his gut mixed with sobs. The hammering on the
dashboard is causing trouble, the wipers are going faster than a fast
thing, lights are flashing like they're on a Christmas tree.

When this is over, I still have to get us home. Please don't break
the car. I can't imagine you sitting still, waiting for the breakdown
service. please… please… oh God!

He lists his crimes, and I recognise most of them: blinding the eyes
on the canvas, trampling the babies on the floor, squishing the frog,
contaminating the tree, 'borrowing' a traffic cone…
I don't know what to say. He is innocent as an infant.
My eyes fall on the tiny print tacked over the fuel gauge: Van Gogh's
sunflower. It whispers a single word: *understate*.

Well son, I don't think you're a saint, but you're not evil.
There is nothing we need to forgive.

The Long Haul

Two climbers begin their descent. Too far from base, the weather has turned.
Their path avalanched, they need a new route down.

My son stands on one leg, immobile, for nearly an hour, eyes staring
into the distance, breath gasping like an old man running after a bus.

The mountaineers reach a small plateau where they rest for the night. They nail
their tent into the ice against the wind, boil snow to hydrate dried rations.

It has been too long, and so I risk touching my son's face, calling his name,
shouting. When he hears, a sudden fright of recognition, and he runs.

The climbers will take days to reach the bottom. Harnessed to each other at their waists,
if either falls, the other must hold, or they will sink together, lost on the rocks.

In the garden, my son howls like a wolf baying the moon, streams of gibberish.
He pulls his hair, clutches a tree, tugs, shakes it. Neighbours peer through curtains.

Descending, they have lost track of time, of how often one slipped, hung from a precipice,
both lives held in the tired grip of the other. They move on, dogged, beyond thought.

I watch him lie where he has fallen. He sleeps there, with the suddenness of an infant.
The madness has left him for now. I place a blanket, sing lullabies, whisper prayers.

They stagger from the mountain's base, stare back at where they've been. Years later
they will sit in bars, tell the tale to youths. Few will venture as far as they, fewer return.

Now, my son brings me coffee. Earilier, he chopped firewood, gathered berries. We eat
together—rock hard nuts, snowy yoghurt, wild fruit. His eyes smile the colour of summer.

Let the Rooms Be Filled With Light

I like those evenings when
the moon's rays bring enough light
to soften the shadows round his sleep,

but when the night is winter dark
I turn on the lamp or burn a candle—
keep the haunting memories at bay:

those years when it seemed he
would always cower in the corners
of crowded rooms, fear wet on his skin—

his smile a razor gash, old spirits
jeering behind his eyes; how he
twitched and jerked, ran from his demons.

I remember the name-callers,
those who feared his oddness, how they
hurried past on the other side of the street.

Tonight I give thanks
for the moon's pale serenity; the slow
tick of the clock, his steady breath, still limbs.

I give thanks for the life of my son,
the end of nightmares, the return of sanity.

the morning opened
to the song of a blackbird
a sunflower lifting

Image Labels

The photographs from the Mother and Son series have no titles, but do have a specific order for exhibitions, listed below together with any additional picture credits:

Page 19:	*Mother & Son # 3*
Page 22:	*Mother & Son # 14*
Page 23:	*Mother & Son # 15*
Page 25:	*Mother & Son # 16*
Page 31:	*Mother & Son # 12*
Page 37:	*Mother & Son # 28*
Page 39:	*Mother & Son # 5*
Page 40:	*Mother & Son # 22* (Camera operator Andreya Hulme)
Page 41:	*Mother & Son # 23*
Page 43:	*Mother & Son # 21*
Page 46:	*Mother & Son # 29*
Page 47:	*Mother & Son # 30*
Page 50:	*Mother & Son # 24*
Page 51:	*Mother & Son # 25*
Page 52	*Mother & Son # 26*
Page 58:	*Mother & Son # 6*
Page 59:	*Mother & Son # 7*
Page 63:	*Mother & Son # 19*
Page 71:	Aidan's Painting—*Klimt-style*
Page 83:	*Mother & Son # 20*
Page 88:	Father & Sone (Photo courtesy of Louise Monique)